FAND💘M FEVER

Beyoncé's
BEYHIVE

BY VIRGINIA LOH-HAGAN

45th Parallel Press

Published in the United States of America by
Cherry Lake Publishing Group
Ann Arbor, Michigan
www.cherrylakepublishing.com

Reading Adviser: Beth Walker Gambro, MS, Ed., Reading Consultant, Yorkville, IL
Book Designer: Joseph Hatch

Photo Credits: © Kristina Kokhanova/Alamy Stock Photo, cover, title page;
© Featureflash Photo Agency/Shutterstock, 4; © frescomovie/Shutterstock, 7;
© Featureflash Photo Agency/Shutterstock, 8; © Francis Specker/Alamy Stock Photo, 11;
© Everett Collection/Shutterstock, 12; © arvzdix/Shutterstock, 13; © andersphoto/
Shutterstock, 14; © Tinseltown/Shutterstock, 17; © arvzdix/Shutterstock, 19; © Sky
Cinema/Shutterstock, 21; © A.RICARDO/Shutterstock, 22; © Featureflash Photo Agency/
Shutterstock, 25; © Abaca Press/Alamy Stock Photo, 26; © Chris Pizzello/ASSOCIATED
PRESS, 29; © A.RICARDO/Shutterstock, 31

Copyright © 2025 by Cherry Lake Publishing Group

All rights reserved. No part of this book may be reproduced or utilized in any form or
by any means without written permission from the publisher.

45th Parallel Press is an imprint of Cherry Lake Publishing Group.

Library of Congress Cataloging-in-Publication Data

Names: Loh-Hagan, Virginia, author.
Title: Beyoncé's Beyhive / Virginia Loh-Hagan.
Description: Ann Arbor : 45th Parallel Press, 2024. | Series: Fandom fever | Audience:
    Grades 4-6 | Summary: "Beyoncé's Beyhive provides an inside look at the powerful
    fandom of Beyoncé. Readers will get hooked on this hi-lo title, covering facts about
    and insights into the group of fans who aren't afraid to make their support of the
    Queen Bee known"— Provided by publisher.
Identifiers: LCCN 2024009602 | ISBN 9781668947449 (hardcover) | ISBN 9781668948835
    (paperback) | ISBN 9781668950357 (ebook) | ISBN 9781668954911 (pdf)
Subjects: LCSH: Beyoncé, 1981—Juvenile literature. | Popular music fans—Juvenile
    literature.
Classification: LCC ML3930.K66 L65 2024 | DDC 782.42164092—dc23/eng/20231212
LC record available at https://lccn.loc.gov/2024009602

Cherry Lake Publishing Group would like to acknowledge the work of the Partnership for
21st Century Learning, a Network of Battelle for Kids. Please visit Battelle for Kids online
for more information.

Note from publisher: Websites change regularly, and their future contents are outside
of our control. Supervise children when conducting any recommended online searches
for extended learning opportunities.

Printed in the United States of America

Table of Contents

CHAPTER ONE
From Fan Base to Fandom 5

CHAPTER TWO
Fanning Beyoncé 9

CHAPTER THREE
Living That Fan Life 15

CHAPTER FOUR
The Power of Fandom 20

CHAPTER FIVE
Insider Information 24

Glossary 32
Learn More 32
Index 32

Dr. Virginia Loh-Hagan is an author and educator. She is currently the Director of the Asian Pacific Islander Desi American (APIDA) Center at San Diego State University and the Co-Executive Director of The Asian American Education Project. She lives in San Diego with her very tall husband and very naughty dogs.

Beyoncé loves her fans. They are called the BeyHive.

CHAPTER ONE

From Fan Base to Fandom

Musicians make music. They perform music. Some become big stars. They become **celebrities**. Celebrities are famous. They have a **fan base**. A fan base is a group of supporters.

Most fans have a casual interest. But some fans are more devoted. They worship their **idols**. Idols are big stars. Devoted fans form **fandoms**. Fandoms are communities. They're networks of fans.

Fandoms of musicians are special groups. They buy the musicians' music. They buy their **merch**. Merch means merchandise. It means stuff that can be sold. Merch includes shirts and posters. Fans follow musicians on tour. They attend their shows. They go on tour with them. They connect with the music. They connect with the messages. They sing their songs. They know all the words.

Fandoms are a powerful force. They can influence music. They use the internet. The internet gives fans information about their idols. It gives them more access to their idols. It also gives them more access to other fans.

Fans build relationships with each other. They share their knowledge. They share their passion. They build connections. They create content. They share content.

Fans make fan art. This is when they draw pictures of their idols. Fans also write stories about their idols. This is called fan fiction. They share their art. They share their stories.

Some celebrities have large fandoms. Their fandoms even have special names. That's a sign of success!

Beyoncé has fans all over the world. She has done 9 tours during her solo career.

Beyoncé is also an actor. She starred in the movie *Dreamgirls*.

CHAPTER TWO

Fanning Beyoncé

Beyoncé Giselle Knowles-Carter was born in 1981. She's super famous. She's known by one name. She's called Beyoncé.

Beyoncé is one of the greatest singers of all time. She's a role model for women. She's a role model for people of color. She was part of a band. The band was Destiny's Child. Then she went **solo**. Solo means performing alone.

Her songs are top hits. She performs all around the world. Her shows sell out. She always has big crowds. She's sold many albums. She's won many awards. She has the most Grammy music awards of any artist. Beyoncé is loved by many.

Beyoncé is called "Queen Bey." It's a play on words of the term "Queen Bee." Queen bees rule a beehive. Beyoncé's fandom is known as the BeyHive.

A Beyoncé fan group started online in the early 2000s. It had online forums. It was first called Beyoncé World. Someone posted a picture of Beyoncé. The picture was inappropriate. Fans got mad. They left that group. They formed a new group.

Fans called themselves The Beyontourage. This combined two words. The words are Beyoncé and **entourage**. Entourage refers to a group of people. These people support a famous person.

A new forum started. It stuck. It was the BeyHive. It has more than 17,000 members. This happened in 2012. Beyoncé liked the name. She supported it.

Beyoncé had a stage name. She called herself "Sasha Fierce." This name helped her with stage fright.

SUPER FAN

Barack Obama was the 44th U.S. President. He's a Beyoncé fan. He was elected president twice. He had a grand ceremony. This happened in 2009 and 2013. Both times, Beyoncé performed. In 2009, she sang "At Last." In 2013, she sang "The Star-Spangled Banner." Barack Obama shares a playlist every year. He often includes Beyoncé's songs. He said, "Beyoncé could not be a better role model for my girls." Barack Obama's wife is Michelle Obama. Michelle Obama is also a fan of Beyoncé. She said, "Hey, Queen! Girl, you have done it again, constantly raising the bar for us all and doing it flawlessly. I'd say I'm surprised but I know who you are. I've seen it up close and personal. Girl, you make me so proud, and I love you." Michelle Obama said if she could be anyone other than herself, she'd be Beyoncé.

Beyoncé rarely gives interviews. But she interacts with her fans. She keeps her projects secret. But she sends clues. She shares pictures. She shares video clips. A fan said, "We get a little bit of information, but not too much." The BeyHive shares news about Beyoncé. They buy her music. They host viewing events. They support Beyoncé.

Beyoncé rarely speaks out against her haters. The BeyHive do that for her. Her fans defend her. A fan said, "She's not going to say anything. So we decided we will. We just got stronger and more vocal."

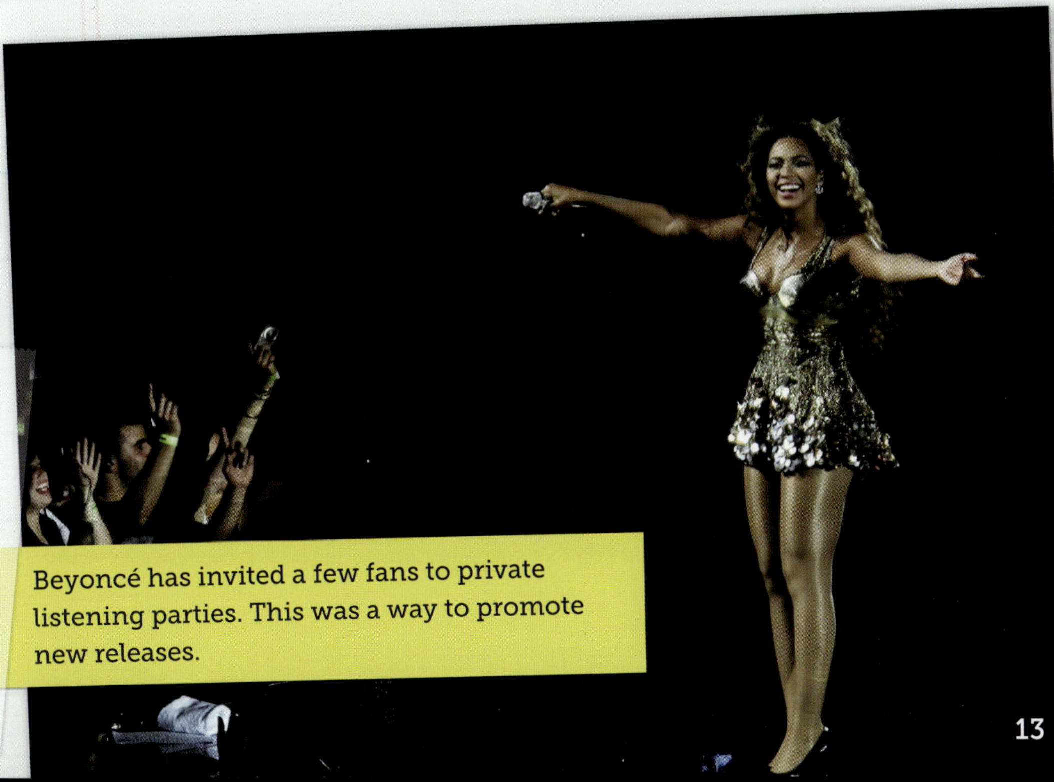

Beyoncé has invited a few fans to private listening parties. This was a way to promote new releases.

Beyoncé once asked fans to wear silver. This was in honor of her birthday. Stores ran out of silver clothes.

CHAPTER THREE

Living That Fan Life

The BeyHive show up at Beyoncé events. To be a fan, make sure to look the part! Do the following:

- Wear **statement pieces**. These items stand out. They draw attention. Some fans wear cowboy hats with face fringe. Some wear bodysuits. Some wear tall boots. Some wear flashy jewelry. Some wear fancy tights.

- Wear gold and silver. Metal colors are popular among Beyoncé fans.

- Wear concert shirts. Each Beyoncé show has merch. Buy shirts. Collect them.

- Wear yellow and black. Those are bee colors.

The BeyHive has their own culture. To be a fan, make sure to act the part! Do the following:

+ Be loyal. Fans support Beyoncé. They honor Queen Bey. They speak out for her.

+ Be active online. Fans are on all social media sites. They keep talking about Beyoncé. They make sure she's trending.

+ Do the mute challenge. "Energy" is one of her songs. Beyoncé sings, "Look around everybody on mute." Fans go silent when she sings this line of the song.

+ Make fan art. Create pictures of Beyoncé. Post them on social media.

Beyoncé fans wait for her to drop her music.

Fanatic Fan

Kid Rock is an American singer. His real name is Robert James Ritchie. In 2015, he did an interview. He said negative things about Beyoncé. He didn't understand her hype. He doesn't get why she's "the biggest thing on Earth." He doesn't think much of her songs. He also commented on her looks. He said that she doesn't "do much" for him. Beyoncé didn't respond. However, the BeyHive stung back. The fans got mad. They swarmed. They posted on all his social media. They posted bee emojis. They're used in electronic messages. The BeyHive flooded his sites with bees. Kid Rock responded. He posted a picture of bug spray. Fans kept up this war. They've sent bee emojis every year. The BeyHive hates haters.

Not all fan behavior is good. Some fans can be **toxic**. Toxic means harmful. To be in the BeyHive, don't let your passion become poison. Do the following:

+ Respect Beyoncé's privacy. Toxic fans have stalked her. They find her. They swarm her.

+ Don't attack people. In 2019, a woman talked to Beyoncé's husband, Jay-Z. Jay-Z's real name is Shawn Corey Carter. This was at a basketball game. Toxic fans targeted the woman. They bullied her. They sent her death threats.

+ Don't mess with Beyoncé's show. This happened in 2018. It was the On the Run II tour. Beyoncé was in Atlanta. A drunk fan hopped on stage. He chased after Beyoncé. He was caught.

People have a right to live their lives. Focus on the art more than the artist.

Beyoncé fans are very protective of her. Protect, but respect!

CHAPTER FOUR

The Power of Fandom

The BeyHive is inspired by their idol. They support her. They support her causes. Together, they're a powerful force. They've helped people. They've made social changes.

Beyoncé supports the Black community. She uses her star power. She doesn't just want sales. She urges her fans to take action. She supported Black Lives Matter. She said, "Let's remain aligned and focused in our call for real justice." She also said, "No more senseless killings of human beings. No more seeing people of color as less than human. We can no longer look away." She asked her fans to pray for peace, compassion, and healing. She has also asked her fans to vote.

Beyoncé uses her fame to help other people.

In 2013, Beyoncé created BeyGOOD **foundation**. Foundations are organizations. They provide money. They support good causes. BeyGOOD supports Black-owned businesses. The foundation has donated millions of dollars.

Beyoncé released a surprise song. It was called "Black Parade." It celebrates Black culture. The BeyHive bought the song. Money from the song supported BeyGOOD.

Sometimes, people have a hard time getting jobs. Beyoncé wanted to help. Goodwill is a company that provides services to people in need. They provide job training. Beyoncé teamed up with Goodwill. She donated money to them. She asked her fans to help. The BeyHive donated clothes. They donated electronics. They helped people look for jobs.

Beyoncé said, "Being Black is your activism. Black excellence is a form of protest. Black joy is your right."

Idol Inspiration

Even idols have idols. Beyoncé admires Michael Jackson. Jackson lived from 1958 to 2009. He was a superstar. He's called the King of Pop. He's known all around the world. He's one of the best-selling artists of all time. At age 5, Beyoncé went to her first concert. She saw Jackson. She was awed by him. She fell in love with performing. She said she discovered her purpose. In 2006, she presented him with an award. She said, "If it wasn't for Michael Jackson, I would never ever have performed." In 2014, people honored Jackson's life. Beyoncé could hear soul in Jackson's music. She said, "Michael Jackson changed me and helped me to become the artist I am." Jackson's son is named Prince. Prince said Beyoncé is the closest artist to match his father. He said, "I know my dad idolized her as well…he saw that same fire and dedication in her."

CHAPTER FIVE

Insider Information

Fans know their idols. They can also spot fake fans. Make sure you do your research. Here are top 10 things every true BeyHive member should know about Beyoncé!

1. Beyoncé is from Houston, Texas. She started singing at an early age. She competed in local talent shows.

2. Beyoncé was on *Star Search*. She was 12 years old. She was part of a band named Girl Tyme. They came in second place.

3. Beyoncé has a famous family. Her husband is Jay-Z. Jay-Z is a rapper. Her sister is singer Solange Knowles. Beyoncé and Jay-Z have 3 children. Blue Ivy is the oldest. She's also a singer. The other children are twins Rumi and Sir.

Beyoncé is married to Jay-Z. They have 3 kids.

Beyoncé and Jay-Z have IV tattooed on their ring fingers. IV is four in Roman numerals. It also matches their first daughter's name, Blue Ivy (IV).

4. Four is her favorite number. Her birthday is September 4. Jay-Z's birthday is December 4. Her mother's birthday is January 4. Her wedding was on April 4. *4* is the name of her fourth album.

5. In 2009, Beyoncé did a show. Her lighting crew made a mistake. She sang, "Lights! Somebody's getting fired, hey hey!" The BeyHive says this when people fail to meet high standards.

6. Beyoncé released a surprise drop. This happened in 2013. It was at midnight on Friday, December 13. The album was called *Beyoncé*. It was released all at once. Fans stayed up late to hear the whole album.

7. Beyoncé started Ivy Park in 2016. Ivy Park is a clothing line. It sells sporty clothes. Famous people and fans buy it.

8. Beyoncé loves art. She visits the Louvre museum. This is a famous place in Paris, France. She did a music video at the Louvre in 2018. After, the museum had more than 10 million visitors.

9. Beyoncé performed at Coachella. This is a popular music festival. Beyonce was the first Black woman to headline. She did this in 2018. Fans called it "Beychella."

10. Beyoncé raises bees. She has 2 beehives. She said, "I have around 80,000 bees. And, we make hundreds of jars of honey a year."

There's so much more to learn! Make sure to keep up with the latest.

In 2024, Beyoncé released an album. It is called *Cowboy Carter*.

Fans have their own language. Here are some BeyHive words you should know:

+ **Beyhydration:** This word rhymes with dehydration. Dehydration means lacking water. Beyhydration describes dry periods. It's when Beyoncé doesn't have any new music out.

+ **Chart Hive:** Fans study music charts. They see which songs become hits. They monitor Beyoncé's standing. They see how she ranks. They compare her to other artists.

+ **Digger Bees:** Digger bees are worker bees. They're like journalists. They search the internet. They learn all they can about Beyoncé. They look for and share new information.

+ **Eras:** These are periods when Beyoncé releases new music.

+ **Honeybees:** Honeybees are the most peaceful fans. They praise Beyoncé. They write positive comments on fan pages.

+ **Killer Bees:** Killer bees target haters. They attack people who criticize Beyoncé.

+ **Wasps:** Wasps are critics. They're considered haters. They say negative things about Beyoncé.

+ **Yellowjackets:** Yellowjackets are Beyoncé fans who only seem to be fans sometimes. Real fans look down on them. They say they're not loyal.

Beyoncé loves her fans. They backed her 2024 album. Critics said *Cowboy Carter* wasn't country enough. One song was "TEXAS HOLD 'EM." It was a hit. It was number one. Beyoncé said "I feel honored to be the first Black woman with the number one single on the Hot Country Songs chart. That would not have happened without the outpouring of support from each and every one of you."

There are all types of Beyoncé fans. BeyHive members are all around the world. Start your own fan club!

- Promote your fan club.
- Collect a list of names.
- Plan events.
- Host a meeting.
- Have fun!

Beyoncé has been the highest-paid woman in music.

GLOSSARY

celebrities (suh-LEH-bruh-teez) well-known or famous people

entourage (ahn-tuh-RAHZH) group of people who travel with or work for an important or famous person

fan base (FAN BAYSS) group of fans for a particular sport, musical group, or celebrity

fandom (FAN-duhm) subculture, community, or network of fans who share a common interest

foundation (fown-DAY-shuhn) organization that provides financial support for activities and groups

idols (EYE-duhlz) people who are greatly admired and loved by others

merch (MURCH) short for merchandise, which includes posters, shirts, and other items

solo (SOH-loh) performing alone, rather than part of a group

statement pieces (STAYT-muhnt PEE-suhz) clothing or accessories that stand out or draw attention

toxic (TAHK-sik) harmful

LEARN MORE

Beyonce. Newport Beach, CA: Saddleback Educational Publishing, 2015.

Moss, Caroline. *Work It, Girl: Beyoncé Knowles: Rule the music scene like Queen.* London, England: Frances Lincoln Children's Books, 2021.

Oswald, Vanessa. *Beyonce: The Reign of Queen Bey.* New York, NY: Lucent Press, 2019.

INDEX

acting, 8
activism, 20–22

bees, 28–30
BeyGOOD Foundation, 22
Beyoncé
  BeyHive interaction, 10, 13, 20, 31
  biography and personal life, 9, 19, 24–28
  photos, 4, 7, 8, 11, 13, 17, 19, 21, 22, 25, 26, 31
  talents, 8, 9, 20, 24, 28
Black Lives Matter, 20
Black pride and joy, 22

concerts, 7, 11, 13, 19, 27, 28
criticism, 13, 18, 30
culture, 15–16, 20, 22, 30

Destiny's Child, 9

famous fans, 12, 23
fandoms, 4–7, 10, 31
fashion, 14–15, 27

Goodwill, 22

Jackson, Michael, 23
Jay-Z, 19, 24–26

Kid Rock, 18

merchandise, 5, 15

Obama, Barack and Michelle, 12

social causes, 20–22

toxic behavior, 19

vocabulary, 30